Memories of

TIN TOWN

The navvy village of Birchinlee and its people

by

Professor Brian Robinson,

M.Sc., Ph.D., D.Sc., F.R.S.C.

First published 2001

Second edition 2010

Dedication

To the memory of Roger, my brother and a fellow Birchinlee aficionado,

and our mother, Violet Mary (née Green), a Birchinlee baby.

ISBN 978-0-901100-88-7

The author's mother, Violet Mary Green, as an infant with her younger sister, Lily, inside their home at hut number 52 in "Top Row" at Birchinlee.

▭▭ Workmen's huts for up to ten
single men, a hut-keeper and
his wife and family

▭▭ Foremen's huts

▭▭▭ Huts for married workmen

═══ Course of the present road

╥╥╥ Level of the Derwent Reservoir
when full

1. Home of the author's mother
2. Accident and general hospital
3. Village coal store
4. Waste incinerator
5. South western extremity of Abbey
Field, the village sports ground

6. Railway siding serving the village
7. Recreation hall
8. School *(and mission room)*
9. School playsheds
10. School playground *(left-hand side
for boys and right-hand side for girls)*
11. Schoolmaster's house
12. Allotment gardens
13. Greengrocer's shop
(Tenant: George Sweet)
14. Clothier and draper
(Tenant: Harry Oliver)
15. Cobbler and hairdresser *(First
tenants: Knowles brothers and Daniel)*

16. Post Office
(Tenant: Mrs. Hebzabad Clark)
17. Grocery shop and bakery
(Tenants: the Gregory brothers)
18. Public bath-house
19. Derwent Canteen
20. Rolling-way from the station platform
to the Derwent Canteen cellar
21. Railway station platform
22. The Bamford & Howden Railway
23. Sweet and tobacco shop
(Tenant: Miss Bessie Bateman)
24. Missioner's house
25. Village inspector's house

26. Police station
27. Isolation hospital
28. Sewage treatment plant
29. Ouzelden bridge
30. Ouzelden railway viaduct
("the gantry")
31. Sutton's Corner on the present road
32. Present private road to
gamekeeper's house
33. Gamekeeper's house
(erected 1909-10 and still in use)
34. Railway bridge over Birchinlee Lane
35. Swing bridge

Birchinlee village, looking westward from the opposite side of the Derwent Valley, as it appeared on July 20, 1904. At this time, the upper cul-de-sac and its three terraces of huts still had not been built. The photograph clearly shows the recreation hall (centre) and the village school above it to the right. The valley bottom is now flooded by the Derwent Reservoir, and much of the former site of the village is now under trees.

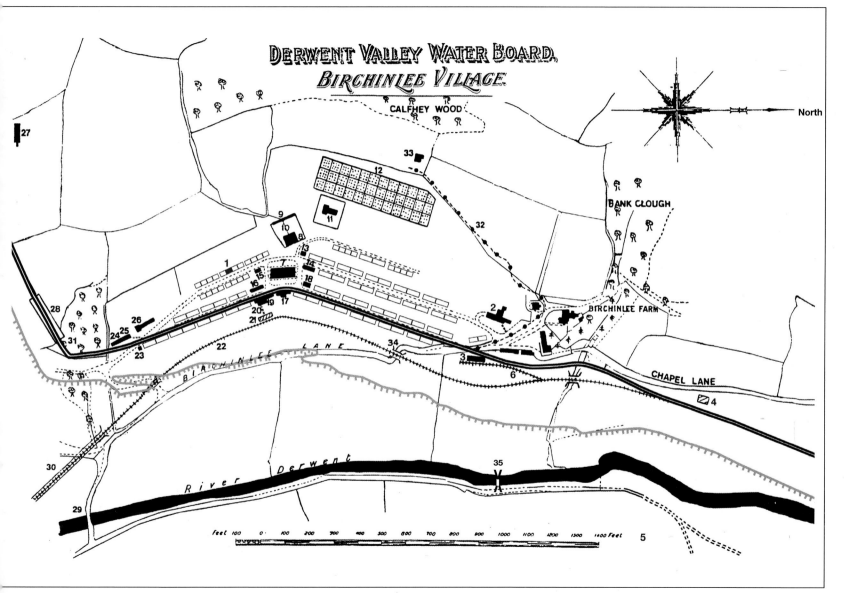

DERWENT VALLEY WATER BOARD,
BIRCHINLEE VILLAGE.

CALFHEY WOOD

BANK CLOUGH

BIRCHINLEE FARM

BIRCHINLEE LANE

CHAPEL LANE

River Derwent

North

Feet 100   0   100   200   300   400   500   600   700   800   900   1000   1100   1200   1300   1400 Feet

5

The Ghost Village

Hidden among the trees on the western side of the Derwent Reservoir in the beautiful Upper Derwent Valley lies the abandoned site of one of the strangest villages in the Peak District.

Its population of nearly 1,000 was purely nomadic and its buildings were single-storeyed with both their green-painted outside walls and black roofs made of corrugated iron, earning it the nickname of either "Tin Town" or "Tin City". Corrugated iron was chosen as the cheapest material for construction, but the interiors of all the terraced bungalows were lined with wood and fitted with classic "Derbyshire" coal-burning grates to withstand the rigours of a Peak District winter at an altitude of 800 feet. This self-contained village had its own shops, school, public house, hospital, recreation hall, and police station. But within 15 years of its foundation, this odd settlement was demolished, and its residents were scattered far afield.

The correct name for this village was Birchinlee, after the old farmhouse which formerly stood at its northern end. It was built mainly between 1901 and 1902 by the Derwent Valley Water Board (DVWB) to accommodate some of its workmen, and their wives and children, who, between 1901 and 1916, built the Howden and Derwent Dams.

These two structures - which at the time of their completion were the two largest masonry dams in the country - were built to impound reservoirs, as they still do, to help meet the requirements for water of the five authorities represented on the DVWB. The Board was incorporated by the inaugural Derwent Valley Water Act of 1899, and

The interior of Tin Town "huts" was surprisingly luxurious. Here a couple of ladies take afternoon tea in front of their classic polished "Derbyshire" grate, with which all the huts were equipped.

had a total membership of 13 which included representatives from the corporations of Derby, Leicester, Nottingham and Sheffield, and the county of Derbyshire. The total amount of water available was 33 million gallons (150 million litres) a day. The component scheme of works, which was to be modified by further Derwent Valley Water Acts in 1901 and 1904, was to involve the building of dams in the Upper Derwent and Ashop valleys to supply water to the five authorities, and was to be effected in three instalments.

The first of these involved the construction of the Howden and Derwent Dams and a supply aqueduct, including a filtration plant at Bamford and a service reservoir at Ambergate.

Although work on the delivery system was carried out under five separate contracts under the overall control of the DVWB, the construction of the two dams was carried out by the Board's own employees. This labour force was drawn mainly from navvies - a name which had evolved from "navigators", the workmen who had been responsible for the digging and construction of the navigations (canals) of earlier times.

With their families, these men were estimated in 1908 to number about 100,000 throughout the country. They moved about from one public work to another as a distinct class or tribe, separated by habit and circumstance from the rest of the community and forming an itinerant labour force which was subject to widespread flagrant abuse by employers.

For example, in the early days of railway construction in this country, the accommodation available to these large numbers of migrant workers and their families was either disgraceful or non-existent, and little, if any, attention was paid to their physical, educational, moral and spiritual welfares. Whole families often found themselves living in squalid conditions which often caused considerable illness, in structures built by the navvies themselves from loose stones and mud and using either ling or heather for roofing. All this was often on very high and exposed ground in the bitterly cold winter months.

Moreover, the contractors also either kept or let provision stores which charged exhorbitant prices for either poor quality or even rank bad food to the labour force, who were captive customers on sites which were usually distant from other centres of population.

Such were the conditions which applied during the driving of the two tunnels between Woodhead and Dunford Bridge north of the Derwent Valley on the former Manchester to Sheffield railway line between 1839 and 1862, where there was gross mismanagement, with the navvy generally being regarded as expendable by those in authority. Although a select committee published a report in July 1846 on the conditions which applied here, Parliament dragged its feet over the introduction of the necessary social reforms.

Nevertheless, something appears to have stirred after half a century because, under Section 64 of the Derwent Valley Water Act of 1899, the DVWB had a statutory obligation to provide a satisfactory environment for the care and accommodation of its employees. The Board admirably fulfilled these responsibilities when it constructed and operated its workmen's village of Birchinlee, in between and close to its dam construction sites. The settlement also installed a degree of social control over the residents and, by thus moulding the behaviour of its workforce, the Board probably improved the former's motivation and efficiency and thereby maximised work output and, ultimately, profit.

The village was laid out along two through roads which were pitched with stone, metalled, kerbed with footpaths and illuminated by means of paraffin-burning lamps – a regular dusk-time sight was the village street lamp lighter, Tom Fletcher, on his round – attached to the roadside buildings. These latter were mainly the "huts", as the domestic accommodation was called, which were of three types – semi-detached workmen's quarters which could take from eight to 10 single men as lodgers along with the hut-keeper, his wife and family; smaller huts in blocks of four which were suitable for married couples with children; and small semi-detached huts for foremen, the weekly rents for which, inclusive of rates, taxes and an average allowance of 3cwt of coal per week, were 10s 6d, 6s 6d and 7s 6d, respectively.

The water supply for the village was obtained from a reservoir impounded in nearby Bank Clough, with gravity-fed supply pipes laid beneath the roadway to service fire appliances and to take water into the huts. These were also serviced by water toilets, still an unusual feature in the early 20th century, which were in separate buildings to the rear of the huts, each row of back-to-backs sharing a toilet building between them.

The nearest city, Sheffield, was 15 miles away and the nearest railway station, at Bamford, was seven miles distant. However, many young people in Birchinlee possessed bicycles and it was also possible to get to and from Bamford three or four times a day using free passes on the Bamford & Howden Railway, a standard-gauge single track with passing loops laid by the DVWB up the western side of the Upper Derwent Valley, primarily to transport building materials to the dam construction sites from the Midland Railway, via Waterwork's Sidings where there was also a platform on which passengers could alight for the short walk to either Bamford (for shopping) or Bamford Station (for onward transit via the Midland Railway to either Sheffield or Manchester).

Looking more like a Wild West saloon, the Derwent Canteen was the only building licensed to sell liquor in the village.

Nevertheless, the village was remarkably self-contained, and had good quality shops including a grocer, green-grocer, tailor, bootmaker, draper and barber. To obviate the shopkeepers' monopoly, hawkers and other travelling tradesmen, among whom were four competing butchers, were permitted into the village.

There was also a public house – the Derwent Canteen – run by the People's Refreshment House Association Ltd.; a school, opened by the Board in 1902 but taken over within a year by the Derbyshire Education Committee; a public bath-house; a post office; an accident and later general hospital and, on the outskirts of the village – about 500 metres up Ouzelden Clough and on its northern lower slopes, an isolation hospital.

The social life of the village revolved around the recreation hall, which was provided with two Riley tables for billiards, a well-stocked library – from which any of the workmen and their families could borrow books – financed from the profits from the Derwent Canteen, which also partially subsidised social functions. Particularly popular among these were the concerts presented by the village children, and others included whist drives, dances, hand-cranked film shows, and an annual horticultural show for produce grown in the allotment gardens on the bank at the western edge of the village.

The coronation of Edward VII was marked by a grand parade, tea party, and sports day on the Abbey Field which became an annual event and one of the highlights of the village year. No sports day was considered complete without the landladies' race, held for the hutkeepers' wives only, and the tug-of-war, which was always the subject of keen rivalry between teams from the two dam construction sites.

The Abbey Field also acted as a cricket and football pitch, and although the cricket team, which played in the High Peak League, was maintained throughout the village's existence, the football team enjoyed far greater popularity and success, even producing a second eleven team.

Only the DVWB's employees up to foremen, whose huts were strategically-placed in the village, lived at Birchinlee, the engineers and managerial staff living elsewhere. However, in addition to the workmen, there were a number of other residents whose sole purpose was to provide social services for the villagers. These included the schoolmaster, policeman, village inspector and navvy missioner, who had accommodation fitted with inside toilets and set well away from the workmen's huts (in keeping with this period when society was highly stratified by class), with the last three being built in commanding positions overlooking the approach road at the southern end of the village. This enabled outsiders to be monitored as they entered the village.

The majority of the DVWB's labour force at Birchinlee had previously been employed by Birmingham Corporation on the construction of the Caban Coch, Craig Goch, the submerged Garreg-Ddu and the Pen-y-Garreg Dams in the Elan Valley, near Rhayader in mid-Wales. This is evident from the prevalence of Welsh surnames among the workforce, included in which was the author's maternal grandfather, "Long" George Green, who, just after the turn of the 19th century, moved with his wife and their three children, Robert, George and Walter from Radnorshire into Hut 52 at Birchinlee. Whilst here the author's mother was born on 5 April 1909, to be baptised Violet Mary on the following 17 June in the parish church at nearby Derwent.

In January and November 1905 and May 1906, for the first time the population of the village exceeded 700, 800 and 900 respectively, and it reached a maximum of 967 during August 1909, when the DVWB's total number of employees was 1,907 (having reached a maximum of 2,753 in June 1908). However, the completion of the construction of the Howden Dam during 1912, together with the impending completion of the Derwent Dam, signalled the beginning of the end for Birchinlee.

So what became of it?

During 1912, consideration was given to the possible use of the village after it was no longer required as accommodation for the DVWB's workmen and their families. The demolition of the huts began in December 1913 and, by August 1914, half of them had been dismantled and some had been sold.

In October 1914, the War Office completed arrangements for the purchase of 14 blocks of workmen's huts, four blocks of married workmen's huts, the public bath-house and the recreation hall. These were dismantled and removed between November 1914 and April 1915 to the prisoner of war camp at Lofthouse Park, near Wakefield. Unfortunately, a recent search of this site failed to locate any trace of these buildings. However, some of the huts were sold locally, and one could, until recently, still be found in the hamlet of Abney where it

Some of the navvies who built the dams. This was the "Black Gang", led by charge foreman Edley Albert "Ted" Yates, who is standing third from the left.

served as a meeting hall, while another forms the shell of a hairdressing salon in Edale Road, Hope. Another of the Birchinlee buildings, although of too small a cross-section to have been domestic accommodation, has recently been located at Leadmill in Hathersage, where it is in use as a stable.

As part of the disposal of the contents of the village's buildings, bedsteads, bedding etc., were given to the Hathersage Hospital for Wounded Soldiers in October 1914. The purchasers of furniture, utensils and crockery included some in the locality, and the two billiard tables from the recreation hall were sold to the then newly-opened Bamford Institute in 1912, where they are still in use.

The last people to live in Birchinlee village were the navvy missioner, George Eustace Sutton, and his six children. His wife, Sarah Ann, died in 1907 when she was only 38 years old. During the final phase of their residence before they moved early in 1915 to Leeds, the family were compelled to live in what had been the post office because their own hut had been demolished. Today, the memory of George Eustace Sutton, who made such a significant contribution over so many years to the quality of life for the residents of Birchinlee, lives on in "Sutton's Corner", the name given to the sharp bend in the present road as it enters the village site from the south, just below and adjacent to where he and his family lived.

The most conspicuous remains left on the site today are the red brick remains of the incinerator, used to dispose the village's rubbish, now found on the west side of the road about 100 metres north of the main site, and the walls and outer doorway of the Derwent Canteen's cellar. The foundations of some of the other village buildings can still be discerned, including the terraces on which the huts and, at SK 16359105, the isolation hospital were built, and the foundations of the accident and general hospital, recreation hall, school, schoolmaster's house, police station, and the missioner's and village inspector's houses. Along the eastern extremity of the village the course of the Bamford & Howden Railway can be followed, including the station platform and the course of the rolling-way from there to the doorway into the stone-lined Derwent Canteen cellar.

The stone foundations of the Ouzelden viaduct, together with a few timbers which remain from each end of the structure, become visible when the water level of the Derwent Reservoir falls accordingly, as does the Abbey Field - the former Birchinlee sports ground - and the ruins of Abbey Farm. In times of severe drought, the Ouzelden bridge may also be exposed.

Further afield, the Birchinlee Memorial Cross can be located in the parish churchyard at Bamford, where it was re-erected to act as the headstone for the large communal grave where the unidentified remains of 58 late residents of Birchinlee were re-interred from the

The village from its northern end and looking along the top through road. Some of the outbuildings of Birchinlee Farm are on the left and in the centre is the northernmost of the foremen's huts, no doubt strategically so placed in order that entry into the village from this end could be monitored.

communal graves in Derwent churchyard before the Ladybower Reservoir was first impounded in 1943. Also at Bamford are the former offices of the DVWB which were sold into private ownership in 1987.

Probably the most interesting legacy of Birchinlee is the prevalence of Welsh surnames which survive in today's villages of the Hope Valley, where many of the former navvies settled with the demise of their sub-culture, stifled by the social, moral and spiritual controls imposed in settlements such as Birchinlee, and by the unavailability of other large public construction works. However, the best testament to their time would appear to be the magnificence of the castellated dams and the handsome power of the impounded reservoirs.

To conclude, it is perhaps appropriate to quote the sentiment of 73-year-old Sydney ("Sid") Lloyd, who was born at Birchinlee on 1 June 1910: "It was a marvellous place to live."

"Sweets to the Sweet."
A charming but heavily-posed photograph of Miss Bessie Bateman's sweet shop at Birchinlee. Orginally built purely for the sale of newspapers, this small kiosk later sold tobacco and confectioneries, a fact which made it an obvious favourite with the village children, as can be seen in the picture. Also of interest, since it provides the only evidence for the possible use of electrical power in the village, is the bell-push to the immediate right of the doorframe.

11

The Navvies

The great Gothic castellated towers of the Howden and Derwent Dams are the greatest memorial to the men who built them nearly a century ago. The "navvies" came to Birchinlee from all over Britain, but many direct from building dams either in Devon or in mid-Wales, hence the large number of Welsh names in the village. By the standards of the day, the DVWB was an enlightened employer, providing many facilities for its workmen and their families, and ensuring that they were not forgotten in the festivities when the Howden Dam was officially opened.

Birchinlee Farm, after which Tin Town took its name, as it appeared around 1900. Before its demolition in 1914, it had been tenanted by David Wain, whose family had farmed there for several generations. Stones from the farmhouse were used to construct the pitching at the foot of the Howden Dam to protect the Howden to Derwent aqueduct.

This is the man whose genius created the Howden and Derwent Dams. Lancashire-born Edward Sandeman was appointed engineer to the DVWB on 5 May 1900. He came to Derbyshire from a position as water engineer to Plymouth, where he directed the design and construction of the Burrator Dam. Following the inauguration of the Howden Dam in 1912, he resigned from the DVWB but was retained as a consultant. Sandeman died on 8 February 1959, two months after his 96th birthday.

The author's maternal grandfather, "Long" George Green, is seen here (right) operating the steam crane which is unloading wagons of rubble stone from the DVWB's quarry at Bole Hill, near Grindleford, at the Howden site. Altogether, the construction of the Howden and Derwent Dams used over 1.2 million tons of stone from this quarry, carried to the sites over the Midland and the Bamford & Howden Railways.

Feeding the stone crushers at the Howden site. Again, the complete absence of any safety protection for the workmen is obvious.

Miners at work inside the tunnelled section of the western wing trench for the Howden Dam. Note the lack of any form of protective headgear - safety at work legislation was still in its infancy, and a total of 18 men were fatally injured and many others maimed during the construction of the Howden and Derwent Dams.

Stone masons at work at Howden, with the steam crane in the background. The man wielding the hammer in the foreground is John Creber, a skilled granite mason, originally from Walkhampton in Devon, who had followed Edward Sandeman to Derbyshire after the Burrator Dam project was completed.

13

Some idea of the scale of the excavations for the dams can be obtained from this photograph of workmen, some on ropes, digging out "the wrinkle" (a fault in the rock) on the downstream side of the trench at Howden in June 1903. Note the highly unstable and loose nature of the rock.

DERWENT VALLEY WATER BOARD.

BIRCHINLEE VILLAGE.

RULES AND REGULATIONS
RELATIVE TO
WORKMEN'S HUTS

RULE 1.---No Lodger to be admitted to a hut without producing a ticket signed by the Doss House-Keeper or a Doctor's Certificate.

RULE 2.---The large dormitory in each hut is designed to accommodate 8 lodgers and must not be occupied by a larger number. Two lodgers may be put in the small room adjoining the Hutkeeper's room if not otherwise occupied. Each Lodger shall be provided with a separate bed.

RULE 3.---Each new occupant of a bed shall be provided with clean sheets, pillow and bolster slips, which shall be changed once a fortnight, or oftener if the Village Superintendent so directs.

RULE 4.---The hut shall be swept out and dusted daily, and regularly scrubbed with hot water and soft soap once a week, or oftener if the Village Superintendent so directs.

RULE 5.---No beer, porter, or other intoxicant shall be permitted in the hut beyond the quantity which each hut-keeper and bona fide lodger is permitted to purchase at the canteen for daily consumption.

RULE 6.---The only lamps permitted in the huts to be safety lamps of approved pattern with metal reservoirs. Any lamps not approved will be liable to confiscation if not removed from the hut after due notice has been given. In the case of hanging lamps a metal or glass bell must be hung over the funnel. The wooden ceiling over the lamps shall be protected by sheet iron, air space being allowed between the plate and ceiling. No oil shall be stored within the hut but shall be kept in the coal store provided for each hut. Petroleum of best quality only shall be used.

RULE 7.---All refuse, ashes. &c. must be emptied into the bins provided for the purpose which must be carried to the edge of the road for collection on such days as the Inspector may appoint. Each dustbin will be numbered with the number of the hut to which it belongs and the hut-keeper will be responsible for the same.

RULE 8.—The tenant undertakes that the sanitary arrangements connected with the hut shall be kept in a perfect state of cleanliness and that he will permit no accumulation of dirt, filth or refuse about the premises. The hut and its appurtenances shall at all reasonable times be open to the inspection of the Village Superintendent or any other official appointed for the purpose by the Board with a view of seeing that the rules and regulations are duly observed, and that the property of the Board is kept in a proper state of cleanliness and repair.

RULE 9.---Any hut-keeper who wishes to be away from his hut for more than one night must first obtain permission from the Village Superintendent who must be satisfied that a responsible person is left in charge of the hut to maintain order during his absence. Any hut-keeper who is discharged from or leaves the works, will be at once required to give up his hut.

RULE 10.—A copy of the above rules shall be posted in the living room of each hut.

RULE 11.—The above rules may at any time be added to or varied by the Board. Infringement of any of the above rules, or any other rules hereafter made, will render the offender liable to notice to quit, and a second offence after warning will be followed by summary ejectment.

By order of the Derwent Valley Water Board.

EDWARD SANDEMAN,
ENGINEER.

Sheffield Independent Press, Limited, 21, Fargate.

"Rules and regulations relative to Workmen's Huts". The actual size of this notice is 17 x 12 inches and a copy was displayed in every hut. It set down the rules governing the functioning of the hut, as laid down by the DVWB. A similar notice, with the obvious exceptions of Rules 1 to 4 and 9, the notable exception of Rule 5, and an additional rule (as Rule 1) that "Tenants are not allowed to receive lodgers into their huts except by special permission from the Engineer obtained by an application through the Village Superintendent", was displayed in each of the married workmen's and foremen's huts.

Workmen walk past the DVWB's on-site office on their way home to Birchinlee from the western side of the Howden Dam construction site. The partially completed dam can be seen in the background.

Navvies wait patiently outside the DVWB's on-site office to receive their weekly wages at the Howden Dam construction site.

The "Pumpsters" at work in the dilapidated-looking corrugated iron pump house at Howden which housed the pumps that removed water from the excavations.

16

The rules and regulations governing the doss house. The actual size of this notice is 17 x 12 inches. It is significant that, unlike the notices posted in the Birchinlee huts, it was considered necessary at this stage to completely prohibit alcoholic drink, and to make a specific reference to expulsion as the result of noisy and disorderly behaviour.

In the left background of this view eastward, across the excavation for the Derwent Dam in September 1904, is the doss house at Hollinclough which was opened in February 1903, on the recently laid upper road on the far side of the valley. All new workmen seeking employment with the DVWB and wishing to live in Birchinlee had to spend a week here, receiving a bath and having their clothes disinfected. Its importance was proved during 1904 when two new workmen were found to be suffering from smallpox, and were taken to the isolation hospital.

The "swing bridge" across the River Derwent, used by workmen from Birchinlee on their walk to work on the central and eastern sections on the Howden Dam construction site, visible in the background. This bridge also provided a pedestrian link from the village to the Abbey Field sports ground, which can be seen in front of Abbey Farm, to the right of centre in the background.

The record stone for the Howden Dam being laid on 21 June 1907 by Thomas Gainsford, chairman of the DVWB, at what was to become the bottom of the west tower of the dam. Immediately to the left of the stone stands Samuel George Hallett, foreman of the Howden site, and to the right is Edward Sandeman, the DVWB's engineer. Children from Birchinlee school can be seen in their Sunday best on the left of the picture and to their immediate right the man with the beard is George Eustice Sutton, the missioner.

The DVWB's workmen, their wives and the shopkeepers from Birchinlee inside an on-site marquee at their celebration tea during the afternoon following the opening of the Howden Dam and after the Board's officials and guests had been entertained to lunch. Whereas the *per capita* cost of the lunch was 13s 6d, that for the tea was only 2s, a disparity which would appear to have been disproportionately high and even the more so since *all* the expenses of the opening were met out of the profits of the Derwent Canteen, namely out of the pockets of the workmen.

Top hat and tails were the order of the day for the opening of the Howden Dam on 5 September 1912. The ceremony was performed by Sir Edward H. Fraser, the chairman of the Derwent Valley Water Board, and the cleric standing to his immediate right rear is Dr. Edwin Hoskyns, the Bishop of Southwell, who led a short religious service on this occasion and during which he gave thanks for the successful completion of this instalment of the scheme and then offered prayers of dedication.

The children of Birchinlee were not forgotten in the celebrations marking the opening of the Howden Dam and are shown here at their celebration tea that was held in the recreation hall. Each child in the village under the age of fourteen years was also presented with a framed souvenir multiple photograph showing the village and the Howden works and reservoir. Other festivities that day included sports, dancing in the recreation hall, and a fireworks display.

Home Life

Living in "huts" with walls of corrugated iron did not mean that the accommodation of the 1,000 residents of Birchinlee was in any sense primitive. Contrary to the general contemporary opinion that the navvies lived in hovels, their homes were actually well-appointed, with wood-lined walls, paraffin-lamp lighting, a "Derbyshire" grate, and furnishings which would not have looked out of place in any middle-class late-Victorian house. Strong family and cultural links are obvious everywhere in these photographs taken inside and outside the houses of the residents of Birchinlee, and what is also evident is a genuine pride in their appearance and the condition of their homes.

A mother proudly poses outside her hut, holding her baby with her daughter by her side. Note the paraffin-burning street lighting which was attached to the buildings. Looking southward, toward the schoolmaster's bungalow, along the minor street (the cul-de-sac), this is the only photograph taken in this part of the village.

A Hogmanay musical evening inside one of the huts. The pipe-player on the right is Edward Kennedy, the gamekeeper who lived at Abbey Grange, a cottage on the opposite side of the River Derwent from Birchinlee. The other piper is his son, William, who married Birchinlee school teacher, Edith Maude Hallett. At the piano is Mr Buchan. Suspended from the ceiling below the decorations is a paraffin lamp, the standard means of indoor lighting throughout the village.

The Yates family, with grandfather in the seat of honour, outside the main entrance to their home at No. 23, Birchinlee. The photograph shows (back row, L to R), Edley Albert "Ted" Yates, Thomas William "Tommy" Yates, Agnes Backhouse (the sister of Mrs. Yates) and Elizabeth "Lizzie" Yates, and (front row, L to R), Bert Yates, Frank Yates, Richard Backhouse (the father of Mrs. Yates), Mrs. Grace Yates (née Backhouse) and Violet Yates.

The Adams family, together with some of their lodgers, in their home at Birchinlee. From left to right at the rear of the table are Mrs Fanny Adams, her sons Alfred William and Jack, _, _, _, and Thomas Adams. At the front of the table are Mrs Adams' niece Fan Craigen and Thomas Henry Adams.

The front of one of the semi-detached workmen's huts situated on the upper side of one of the two through-roads. This photograph gives some indication of the extensive landscaping which was required to create a level building surface. The huts were constructed so that the bedrooms of adjoining properties backed on to one another, ensuring quiet nights.

Mrs. Grace Yates on the lower through road outside No. 23, with her bicycle. The recreation hall can be seen in the left background.

The Caswell family in their home, hut number 17, at Birchinlee. On the front row, from left to right, are Violet, Mrs Caswell, Ernest, Sidney and Emily and, likewise, on the back row are George Caswell, Florence, Harold and Lilly. Behind Mr Caswell is the curtain concealing the entrance to the children's bedroom, at the other side of the fireplace was the entrance to their parents bedroom, and the sleeping accommodation for their lodgers was located through a door in the wall opposite the fireplace.

A young lad, thought to be "Tup-penny" Davis, poses with his pet dog and a neckerchiefed man, holding up a finger as if to keep the boy quiet while the photograph is taken, who is thought to be the family's lodger. Many Birchinlee families took in single workmen lodgers.

The Yates family say goodbye to Birchinlee. This photograph was taken in September 1911 by George Sutton, the missioner, on the day that the Yates family left the village to emigrate to New Zealand. It shows (standing), Mr. Edley Albert Yates and Violet, and in the front row, Tom, Mrs. Grace Yates and Frank.

The wedding party of Edith Maude Hallett, assistant teacher at Birchinlee school and William Kennedy, the gamekeeper's son from Abbey Grange, outside Edith's home at Marebottom Farm on 4 August 1908. The bride's father, Samuel George Hallett, seen with his wife to the left of the groom, was the foreman in charge at the Howden site, and the groom's mother and father are to right of the bride. Centre in the back row is Walter Rouse, vicar of Derwent and chaplain to Birchinlee. At the group's extreme left stands Charles Pickett, the foreman in charge at the Derwent site, and third and fourth from the left in the front standing row are William Arthur Ward Turner the schoolmaster at Birchinlee, and his wife Elgiva.

23

The Buchans, Greenings and Wards share a musical evening inside a Birchinlee hut.

The Bullard family outside their home at No. 25, Birchinlee, along with some of their neighbours and lodgers. Seated on the far left is Mrs. Emeline Bullard, in the centre the accordian player is Thomas Bullard, while to his left, the flute player is George Bullard. His left hand had been amputated when he was 14 years old after it was almost severed by machinery while he was working on a crane. To his left is Suzie Bullard and standing second from the left in the back row is Mr. John Thomas Bullard and standing on the far left of this row is the young Frank Yates from "next door" (hut No. 23).

Washday at Birchinlee - long before the days of either washing machines or launderettes. The women from left to right, are Mrs. Martha Agnes Hicks, Mrs. Fanny Elizabeth Greening and Mrs. George Davies.

The wedding feast of William Henry (Harry) Ashworth and Vinetta Dobson, on Boxing Day 1910. The happy couple are seen seated at the head of the table inside the Ashworth family's home in Birchinlee. A custom at Birchinlee weddings was "roping the road", in which the best man needed a plentiful supply of copper coins in order to pay the "tolls" to allow the wedding party to cross the clothes lines, which would be stretched across the road by villagers at various points between Birchinlee Village and Derwent church.

Shops and Services

Although temporary in nature, Birchinlee, or Tin Town, was a remarkably self-contained and self-sufficient community. In addition to having a wide range of shops and frequent visits by tradesmen and hawkers from outside the valley (but under supervision of officials from the DVWB who wished to circumvent the possibility that the village shopkeepers might have a monopoly), the village had its own school, police station, hospital and isolation hospital, and a "missioner" who looked after the spiritual needs of the residents.

Looking northward circa 1904 from the centre of Birchinlee village along the top through road. In the extreme left foreground is the greengrocery shop and opposite is the tailor's shop tenanted by Harry Oliver, known throughout the village as "Harry the Jew." On 8 August 1904 in the parish church at Derwent, Harry married Miss Mary Ellen Gregory, the sister of the Gregory brothers who were the tenants of the grocery shop. Standing at the extreme right foreground is the schoolmaster, Arthur Charles Pritchard, along with his two daughters, Olive Evans (in the darker dress) and Doris Victoria.

A view from the southern end of the village, looking towards the lower through road (centre) and the upper through road on the left. Miss Bessie Bateman's sweet shop is in the right foreground, and standing with his bicycle is Sgt. MacDonald (known as "Big Mac" because he stood 6ft 5in), the policeman from Ashopton in charge of policing the Upper Derwent Valley. The two horse-drawn carts are typical of the travelling traders who visited the village to sell their wares.

Neil McLean, resident police officer at Birchinlee from 1907 to 1915, stands proudly by his bicycle in a lane near the village. Although not a small man, he was known as "Little Mac" only in comparison with Sgt. MacDonald. Although a cell was provided at Birchinlee police station, it was not used during the first five years of its existence, and was later converted into domestic accommodation for a family.

"Fine Cabbages - Two for 3d" is the caption to this fine photograph of George Sweet's greengrocery shop at Birchinlee. William Motley, seen here on the left of the picture serving a cabbage, was responsible for the day-to-day running of the shop which was tenanted by George Sweet of Sheffield. Motley was known throughout the village as "Dick", the name of his horse which drew the cart bringing the fruit and vegetables to the village each day from Sheffield. On the right of the picture, a freshly-killed rabbit is sold to another villager.

Another view of the greengrocers, carefully posed for the long exposure needed by the photographer. William Motley is seen in the doorway of the shop holding a basket, while a couple of other assistants appear to be having a tug-of-war with customers over two marrows! The village school can be seen on the left of the picture, and the schoolmaster's bungalow on the right, behind a group of navvies.

The fine, gabled exterior of Gregory brothers' grocery shop on the lower of the two through roads at Birchinlee. The Gregorys, who came from Tideswell, had a bakery built at the rear of the building in 1905.

"Will that be all now?" is the caption for this photograph of the well-stocked interior of Gregorys' grocery shop.

John Townsend (left) of Bamford, on his newspaper delivery round at Birchinlee, enjoys a brew on a cold winter's day with Fred Atkinson, who is standing at the door of his hut. George and John Townsend, whose family ran a newsagent's and confectionery shop at Bamford, brought the papers up by train and delivered them throughout the village, despite the fact that they were both almost totally blind.

"Cobbler Bob", the boot and shoe maker and repairer at work inside his cobbler's shop at Birchinlee. He took over this shop from the first tenants, the Knowles brothers and Daniel, in November 1903.

One of the mobile shops which regularly visited Birchinlee, came from Bradwell, some 10 miles away. It was the butcher's shop of Jesse Eyre (the tallest of the two men). It is seen here parked outside what the caption rather grandly calls the "Town Hall and Market Square". The "Town Hall" in the left background is actually the white-painted recreation hall, and the village post office can just be seen behind the two men standing on the extereme left.

Business is brisk as village children gather round the horse-drawn mobile fish-and-chip shop, which came to the village weekly from Sheffield. When not in use it was parked in a recess near the Gregory brothers' grocery shop. Note the track of the Bamford & Howden Railway in the background.

A winter's view of the school at Birchinlee. The school opened on 1 September 1902, when 57 infants and 53 older children were admitted. The school was well-attended and was administrated by the DVWB until September 1903, when it became the responsibility of the Derbyshire Education Committee. An evening school was opened on 30 September 1902 when a total of 28 men and youths enrolled. A fee of 2d. per week was charged to each workman attending the class, this being fully refunded to those workmen who had an attendance record of 75 per cent or more at the end of the session. The curriculum was to include reading and writing, elementary drawing, arithmetic, vocal music, history and ambulance (first aid), the latter subject being of particular practical significance in that it provided "first-aiders" who could be called upon in emergencies on the work sites. The author's mother lived in one of the four huts, indicated on page 5, in the middle block of the top terrace shown beyond the school.

The infants class at Birchinlee school, with its teachers, Sarah Eyre (in the light dress behind the desk at the front of the class) and Edith Maude Hallett to the right. The partitioning screen, used to form two separate classrooms, is seen in the right background.

Charmingly titled "Three Little Maids from School", this photograph shows three of the teachers standing outside the Birchinlee school. From left to right they are Miss Sarah Eyre, Miss Roberts, and Miss Edith Maude Hallett.

HE INFANTS AT DRILL

The children and staff of Birchinlee school, photographed in the boys' playground on 29 April 1907. The schoolmaster (William Arthur Ward Turner) is second from the left on the fourth row, his wife (Elgiva) – the schoolmistress is standing at the far right of the second row, and to his immediate front right stands Miss Sarah Eyre, the infants' teacher who shared these duties with Miss Edith Maude Hallett (on the far left of the seated front row – and the daughter of Samuel George Hallett, the foreman at the Howden construction site) and Miss Roberts (in the high-necked dark dress and standing behind Miss Hallett). The first appointees (from 1 August 1902) as schoolmaster and schoolmistress at Birchinlee were Arthur Charles Pritchard and his wife Sarah Ann. They were followed by the Turners on 1 October 1904 who held the positions until 31 August 1912 when Thomas Perkins took over as headmaster for a year, to be followed by Tom Allen who held the position from September 1913 until the school closed on 30 October 1914.

BAMFORD & HOWDEN RAILWAY.

UP.   **RETURN** | **TICKET.**   **DOWN.**

Issued to _____ | Issued to _____

Date _____ | Date _____

Issued by _____ | Issued by _____

Not available if more than a week old.

The user of this Ticket accepts the same for his or her
personal use only, and engages that the Derwent Valley Water
Board shall not be responsible to him or her, or to his or her
representatives, in the event of any accident or injury happening
to him or her whilst on any portion of the Railway.

Actually measuring 5¼ x 4½ inches and printed in black on an orange-coloured paper is this passenger ticket. These were issued gratis to intending passengers upon application to the DVWB's office at Bamford. One of the connections between the village and the outside world was the DVWB's own railway. Shown here is the open platform on the Bamford & Howden Railway at Birchinlee, with the locomotive "Buller", which was primarily involved in shunting work at the Howden site. This picture shows it on passenger duty however, en-route down the valley with the four-compartment coaches which the DVWB purchased in 1903 to enable their employees and the village residents to use the line between Birchinlee and a platform at "Waterworks' Sidings". The beer barrels are en-route either to or from the cellar of the Derwent Canteen, about 30 yards away, on a rolling-way to the left of the picture. Perhaps the delivery of beer was the foremost reason for the construction of the platform.

The ward in the accident hospital in the summer of 1907. Initially, only men who had been injured at work were admitted for treatment but, eventually, the facility was made available, upon payment of an appropriate fee, to the population of Birchinlee, prior to which medical services had been provided by Herbert Lander, a general medical practitioner from the nearby village of Hathersage. However, when an overtly avaricious Lander soon began during early 1902 to attempt to take financial advantage of this situation, the DVWB advertised for a medical officer at Birchinlee. The first appointee (from 31 March 1902) was John Charles Harcourt, with subsequent holders of the post being Messrs E. Arvan Frear Wilkes (from October 1906), Alfred Leitch (from October 1910) and Stephen Rowland (from June 1912 until late in 1914).

The possibility of the spread of smallpox among Birchinlee's workmen persuaded the DVWB to construct this isolation hospital on the outskirts of the village, on the northern bank of Ouzelden Clough. In the event, the hospital was mainly used for the quarantining of village children suffering from scarlet fever, a contagious disease which was fairly widespread until a few decades ago.

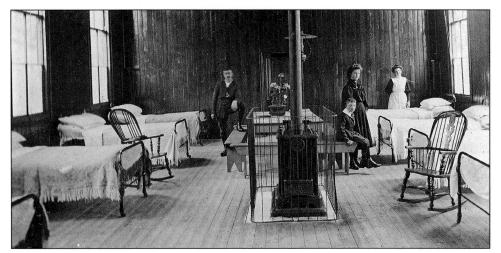

One of the two main works in the isolation hospital at Birchinlee.

There were a total of 66 cases of scarlet fever among the children of Birchinlee between 1902 and 1912, all of whom recovered. A particularly severe epidemic of 26 cases - probably, in part the group shown outside the isolation hospital in this photograph with their ward maids and their nurses - took place in 1905.

Social Life

Birchinlee may have been an isolated community and have had only a short life but this was long enough for the village to develop most of the normal village institutions and so its residents enjoyed a busy and active social life. The Derwent Canteen might have been the only place where the workmen could get a drink, but the recreation hall staged many events which attracted large numbers from inside and outside the village. The Abbey Field was the focal point for the community's sporting activities and the scene of the annual sports day. Derwent parish church was the nearest place of worship, and the beautiful countryside of the Upper Derwent Valley was available for exploration by children and adults alike.

The Derwent Canteen was a popular attraction which led to it being enlarged in 1903 and then further in 1906. Here is seen the works under way on the first extension to the Canteen early in 1903. The portly man seen leaning on his stick on the extreme left of this photograph is Richard Hardwick, the village superintendent. Hardwick was responsible for the maintenance of the huts and other buildings, the collection of rents, the distribution of coal and general cleaning throughout the village. His work as sanitory inspector earned him the nick-name of "Shit-house Dick."

Led by a brass band, the procession leaves Birchinlee en route via Ouzelden bridge, for the Abbey Field for the annual sports day. The sports day was a highlight in the village's social calendar, and was instituted in 1902 to mark King Edward VII's coronation.

Children from Birchinlee enjoying tea in front of Abbey Farm during a Sports Day on the Abbey Field. Bending over handing out cakes in the foreground is Miss Sarah Eyre, the infant teacher and at the rear, in the dark suit and white trilby hat is William Arthur Ward Turner, the schoolmaster, with George Eustace Sutton, the missioner, to his left.

The boys' skipping race at a sports day on the Abbey Field. In the centre background, behind the mound of rubble from the excavations of the foundations of the Howden Dam, can be seen Abbey Grange, the home of gamekeeper Edward Kennedy and his family.

Posing proudly with the medals and the two cups which they won in 1912 is the first team of the Birchinlee Football Club. The team, which played in light blue shirts and white shorts, played their home games at the Abbey Field, and boasted a bulldog mascot which was attired in a similar strip.

The caption says this is the Black Gang versus the "Fat 'Uns" in the Tug-of-War at a Birchinlee village sports day. We have already met the Black Gang, led by Edley Albert "Ted" Yates, on page 9, and are left to wonder if the weight advantage obviously enjoyed by the "Fat 'Uns" would be enough to beat their rivals.

The recreation hall, seen here, served as the main focus for social and community life in the village.

Inside the recreation hall looking toward the stage.

QUIET GAME IN THE "RECK"

Two workmen still wearing their flat caps enjoy a quiet game of billiards in the "reck", as the recreation hall was commonly known.

Some of the village's young men and boys pose rather self-consciously in front of the main entrance to the recreation hall.

Three little girls from Birchinlee pose by the Ouzelden Bridge. Part of the village can just be made out in the middle right background, above the bridge, in this photograph taken around 1910, looking westward.

Some of the younger children in pantomime costume in 1912, with Violet Mary Green (who was to become the author's mother) in the middle of the front seated row of seven children.

The "reck's" parquet floor was ideal for dancing on, and the dances there, notably the Birchinlee Balls, had widespread fame and were attended by an influx of young people, especially females, from areas lower down the valley and in the Hope Valley. Special return trains ran from the platform at "Waterworks' Sidings" to Birchinlee. Music and singing for the dancing was provided either by a visiting dance band and vocalist or by the villagers themselves, with Miss Bessie Bateman, who ran the sweet and tobacco shop, being the resident pianist for such functions. For the balls, the interior of the hall was decorated with flags, Japanese lanterns, bunting and devices of all kinds appropriate to the affair. For example, at those organised by the Ambulance Class, triangular bandages, emergency baskets, and other things associated with the work of the Class would form part of the decorative arrangements.

"The Japanese Fans" is the title given to this group of younger girls from Birchinlee school, posing in concert attire in the boys' half of the school playground.

Workpeople and a few friends met half the cost of the Birchinlee Memorial Cross, the balance being donated by the DVWB out of their profits from the Derwent Canteen. The Cross is shown here, as it stood in Derwent churchyard some 10 yards to the left of the church porch where it marked the 16th communal grave. Of Aberdeen granite and 9ft 6in high, the Cross is beautifully sculptured and its base is inscribed – ERECTED BY D.V.W.B. WORKMEN AND FRIENDS TO THE MEMORY OF THOSE WOMEN AND CHILDREN OF BIRCHINLEE AND OF ALL THE MEN EMPLOYED ON THE CONSTRUCTION OF THE HOWDEN AND DERWENT RESERVOIRS [sic] WHO DIED A.D. 1901-1912.

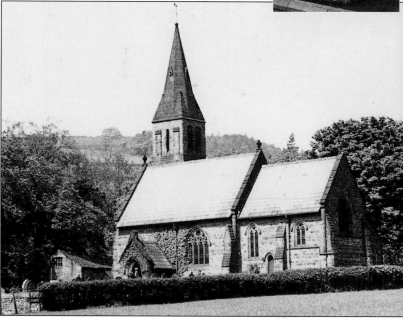

Derwent parish church was where Birchinlee's baptisms, weddings and funerals took place. The site of this church is now beneath the waters of the Ladybower Reservoir. Nearly 100 of Birchinlee's dead were buried in Derwent churchyard, some in private single graves but the majority in adjacent communal graves, 18 in all, which were contained in one long plot beside the churchyard wall on the northwestern side of the church at the rear of the steeple.